THE EMAIL MARKETING CHEAT SHEET

PROVEN EMAIL MARKETING STRATEGIES TO GROW YOUR LIST, CAPTIVATE YOUR AUDIENCE AND EXPAND YOUR BUSINESS

BY SMART READS

I0011342

Free Audiobook

As a thank you for being a Smart Reader you can choose 2 FREE audiobooks from audible.com. Simply sign up for free by visiting www.audibletrial.com/Travis to get your books.

Visit:
www.smartreads.co/freebooks
to receive Smart Reads books for FREE

Check us out on Instagram:
www.instagram.com/smart_readers
@smart_readers

ABOUT SMARTREADS

Choose Smart Reads and get smart every time. Smart Reads sorts through all the best content and condenses the most helpful information into easily digestible chunks.

We design our books to be short, easy to read and highly informative. Leaving you with maximum understanding in the least amount of time.

Smart Reads aims to accelerate the spread of quality information so we've taken the copyright off everything we publish and donate our material directly to the public domain. You can read our uncopyright below.

We believe in paying it forward and donate 5% of our net sales to Pencils of Promise to build schools, train teachers and support child education.

To limit our footprint and restore forests around the globe we are planting a tree for every 10 hardcover books we sell.

Thanks for choosing Smart Reads and helping us help the planet.

Sincerely,

Travis & the Smart Reads Team

TABLE OF CONTENTS

INTRODUCTION

This eBook contains the strategies used to transform an initial 0 to 100-email list into the thousands. It also explains the processes behind using these steps and insights and lessons you can learn along the way.

Does growing your email list really have any impact on your revenue results? Is there such a strong link?

Yes and yes. When you double or triple your email list, it means you double and triple your audience – aka, potential people that could buy your product or avail of your business – hence, its likely you'll double and triple your revenues as well.

Email marketing is an outbound marketing tactic that creates predictable revenue. In other words, once you get going with it, you tend to know how much money it's going to make you from year to year.

A lot of businesses have grown from a small home business, to a six-figure company with office spaces and staff members. While email marketing isn't the sole reason for any business' success, it plays a huge and crucial role.

If you have a strong email marketing list, you probably could climb to the top of Amazon's bestseller list or even earn $2000 in just 10 minutes. That's how powerful an email marketing list can be. It's not alchemy. It's not science fiction. It's a method, and one that's easy to come to grips with.

By turning your attention to emails and growing a large emailing list, you'll not only become a powerful, elite marketer - you'll also become the owner of a business that's growing at an amazing rate.

Let's delve into how to make email marketing work for you.

CHAPTER 1: WHAT ARE THE PROS SAYING?

it's likely you've heard of Seth Godin. If you haven't, he's a marketing god and author who loves permission marketing. It's what you'll be doing, and it converts total strangers into your buddies. Then, it converts these buddies of yours into customers. That sounds sweet, right?

And Seth knows a thing or two about this, since he blogs literally each day. And because his blog posts are emailed to his subscribers, they receive an email each day. He's always in touch with his pals/customers! And they love it.

Turning A Stranger Into A Buddy

This sounds pretty hard to do, huh? Sure, it's easy to stumble into a bar at closing time, drunk, and befriend a fellow drunk who you've never met before.

"Me and him are going to go to Paris together!" you bawl to the bartender, who shakes his head. To turn total strangers into buddies on the Internet, you need something more than mutual intoxication. You need trust.

Trust is the fulcrum to all successful email marketing campaigns. Without it, you can't do anything. With it, you can do whatever you want.

Before you send any emails to your audience, make sure they trust you. Win their favor first.

The Agora Model
You should be aware that your email wouldn't be the only one dropping into your subscriber's inbox. There will be your email, and lots of others - potentially including ones from your competitors. Some people receive a lot of emails each day, and yet you want them to notice yours, and to open it. This can only happen if you're a trusted sender.

Research has demonstrated that most email users trust up to sixteen sources. In other words, that's sixteen sources whose emails they'll open. As for the other sources they don't trust, they might open their emails. But they probably won't. As such, you need to become someone they can trust.

The Agora Model, which is a fancy way of saying, The Organic Model, fast tracks you into becoming a sender people trust. It's a proven method and it actually works.
The following are results of using this model:

• The Agora Model drives organic traffic to your page from all your marketing platforms, such as social media, blogs and paid ads
• Once people arrive on your page, your goal is simple - to get them to subscribe by filing out an easy opt-in form
• How do you get people to opt-in? The easiest way is to offer free stuff
• Once you've got subscribers, start sending regular emails. Make them compelling.
Over time, you can start to market your services and products to them

Whatever your free gift is, make sure it's relevant to the target audience. You wouldn't offer basketball tickets to a sewing circle.

The Power Of Attraction
Your goal is nothing complex. It's super simple: You want people to subscribe. That's it. Once they've subscribed, you can start marketing your products to them.

However, the hard work begins once they've subscribed. At this point, you then need to create a content strategy that wows them each time. You want them to keep opening your emails. In other words, you want them to be so attracted to you that they want more and more from you.

So make sure you send out regular emails that are interesting, engaging, entertaining and informative. Entice them by letting them know what you've got coming up, and how often they can expect to see you in their inbox.

Also, send a "Thank you for signing up" email. It makes you more likeable. And people are inherently attracted to likeable people.

Don't Spam

Before you start emailing folk, you should let them know what to expect. Now that you've done that, you absolutely must not violate this agreement by throwing them a curve ball.

"Hey! I said I was going to email once a week, but I'm actually going to bombard you twice a day with cool stuff you can buy from me!"

Doing the opposite of what you said is actually illegal. It violates the CAN-SPAM act and can land you in trouble. And even if it doesn't, you will lose lots of customers. They will unsubscribe.

So don't be a douche. Deliver emails that will help people. Don't annoy them by emailing them all the time.

Let People Give Feedback

It might sound scary to ask your subscribers to give you feedback. After all, what if they say something you didn't want to hear? You need to develop tougher skin, and put yourself out there. Ask your subscribers, what are they enjoying about your emails? What are they not enjoying? What could be better? Use surveys and polls to get a better idea of what your audience wants from you.

Doing this may be a bit of an eye-opener at first. You might find that your readership has a few issues with your content. In the long term though, it will benefit you, as you can then start to tweak your content so your audience is getting what they want. It's a win-win situation.

Also, asking for feedback shows your audience you genuinely care about them and want to give them content they like. It helps to strengthen the relationship when you reach out to them.

And if you do add any changes as a result of the feedback, name-drop the people who suggested the changes. It will further strengthen the bonds and make people feel like an important part in what you're doing. It will make them feel special.

Shift The Focus From Your Products To Their Interests

Readers prefer to open emails that are based on their specific interests. You got a great product for them? Great! But sometimes that isn't enough for a person to open your emails.

Instead, ask what interests your readers. But how do you know what their interests are? You won't until you ask them. So, go ahead and ask. This works brilliantly. Once you know what your readers want to see from you, you can start to create the right content.

It's called market research, and it's a powerful tool. It means you're not wandering around in the dark, offering things no one wants, and then getting annoyed when they don't buy from you.

The more you involve readers in this, and the more you send emails they actually want to read, the more you became a trusted sender. Which is - after all - the end game here.

You want to offer amazing content. But until you know what people want to see, your quality content will miss the target. It will be excellent, but it won't be what this audience in particular wants to see right now.

Don't Abuse Your Power
They say that with any kind of power comes corruption. Some email marketers get a bit giddy when they swell their list, and start hard-selling their products. It's too good of an opportunity not to take advantage of!

If you abuse your power, though, you erode all the trust you've taken so long to build. Not cool. And once you start to lose all that trust, you might find that people start to unsubscribe in droves.

Along with each message you send, remind people they've already given you permission to be in their inbox. It's polite, and it also does remind them (some people often forget who or what they've subscribed to). You should also include an easy way for them to unsubscribe. Chances are they won't unsubscribe, but it's nice to see you're graceful enough to at least give them the option.

Here are a few things you should also avoid:

1.) Content that isn't relevant or content that's selling someone else's product, or promoting a buddy of yours.

2.) Poor writing. Don't rush. Take your time. If you wouldn't read it, don't send it. Make sure your grammar and spelling is on point, and always put effort into each post. Shoddy writing shows you don't care about your audience, and it's a major turn-off.

3.) Too much info. If you overload people with information and content all the time, they're going to get sick of you.

4.) Broken links. This one is obvious, but it's still one that comes up a lot. Always go back to your emails to make sure any links you've used are still live.

Building an email marketing list isn't just about selling. It's about building a lasting relationship so you become an authority figure in a particular niche, and even a friend to people.

CHAPTER 2: SELLING

The number one reason you want to get into email marketing is because you want to sell more. And, yes, email marketing becomes a valuable business asset once you've got into it. And the good thing is, unlike social media, your email marketing list isn't subject to volatile trends and shifts in usage. It's always under your control, like a cruise liner - as opposed to a dinghy in the middle of the Atlantic Ocean.

As long as you maintain all the effort you're putting into building your emailing list right now, it will remain a valuable business asset for years to come. Unless you do something silly, it's not going to go away. And that's incredibly exciting.

In fact, email marketing is such a powerful tool that our inbox has been called "the hottest social network out there." Once you've reached a stage where people truly trust you, you can't lose. You've got a list of people who are genuinely interested in your content and products. Some will even hang on to every word you say!

Email newsletters allow you to prime your prospects, advertise your wares, and complete any other marketing aim you might have. A big reason for its flexibility is that email can adapt to what is known as the motivating sequence.

The Motivating Sequence
It was writer Bob Bly who first brought the term "motivating sequence" into the mainstream. He highlighted, it was a tried and tested way of generating sales. There are 5 steps that guide a prospect from being a mere prospect into a customer who makes a purchase from you. In essence, it's a sales funnel that always works. Here are the 5 steps:

1.) Grab the attention of your readers with your email newsletter. This often comes in the form of a hook, which is your subject line or an engaging opening line in the email itself. Your hook needs to be catchy, punchy, and it needs to tap into something your reader feels and desires.

2.) Set out a problem your reader has. Your reader is in your list of subscribers - they have a problem that they hope you can solve for them. Are you up to the task? You better be! Don't pussyfoot around the problem. Get right to it. Remind them that they've got an issue.

3.) Once you've highlighted their problem, it's time to focus on the solution. What are you and your company going to do for the reader? How are you going to solve their problem for them? Show them exactly how you're going to make that problem go away.

4.) But hey wait a minute! What if your solution isn't as good as someone else's? Why should people trust you? Outline your USP. Draw attention to what it is that makes your product different from others. What do you offer that no one else has got? You can throw in a few testimonials here, and remind your readers of what they'd be missing out on.

5.) Lastly, include a Call to Action. You've primed your audience. You've got them into a positive state of mind where buying from you has become a real possibility. So, now you've got to clinch the deal by reminding them to buy from you, and showing them exactly where they need to click to make the purchase.

Creating A Buzz
What many email marketers love about emails is they let you create a buzz with your audience.

Let's say you've got a brand spanking new product you're ready to take to market. You can use your emails to give your dedicated readers a sneak preview of this product. If you've got a new book, let them read a chapter. If you've got a webinar coming up, show them exclusive footage of what's going to be in it.

Use your emails to generate excitement among your readers. Pique their curiosity, make them thirsty. Make them so intrigued that they want to hear more.

Employing The Product Launch Tactic
Now that there's a bit of buzz going around about your new product, it's essential you make the most of it by announcing it in your email newsletter.

Customers don't respond well to lots of messages. That's a rule. But you can still use your newsletter to launch an effective marketing campaign that raises awareness of your new product, and gets people interested in it.

A lot of newbie email marketers are often in a mad rush to send out as many emails as possible to their subscribers. They want to get their attention quickly. But this is utterly the wrong way to go about things. It's much better to distribute your content across all your platforms, including email, social media and even video.

Don't go all-in with email marketing. Don't overwhelm your audience. It's a bad move. They'll get sick of hearing from you, and they might unsubscribe.

It's a bit of a balancing act. You want to raise awareness of your product, but you don't want to overwhelm people. Moreover, you don't want to appear as though you're shoving something in someone's face. So what do you do?

It's recommended that you send out a newsletter with a short Q & A that asks what your customers are looking for in a product. What would solve their problems? What is something they would buy?

Essentially, this is a form of market research. You're inviting the customers to tell you what they want, and afterwards you will then happily show them that you have got exactly what the want. How can they not be happy about that?

Your Launch List
Your website doesn't need to have just the one opt-in. It can have two. People are very skeptical about opt-ins because they often assume that people just want to sell stuff to them while bending their ears this week and the next about this and that.

In other words, they don't want to see you in their inbox all the time. Not everyone is skeptical, of course, but a lot of people are.

As such, it's a good idea to have a second opt-in on your website that seems a bit less binding than "sign up for daily or weekly newsletters!" This second opt-in could be something along the lines of, "I want to learn more!"

This is also a good idea because you're creating a group of people who are interested in your product, as opposed to a group of people who want to receive loads of emails from you all year-round.

See, maybe they don't care to receive all those emails. Maybe they're not interested in what you have to say. Maybe they just want to get to the nitty-gritty and learn more about your product.

You could even invite your current subscribers to opt-into this second list. Why not? It's a good way to target your marketing more specifically to people who genuinely want to buy from you.

Once the product has been launched, you should stop using this second list of prospects. They've got all that they signed up for, so it's polite to then just leave them be. Another good tactic businesses use all the time is using your newsletter as a pre-sales tool of sorts.

What this means is you build anticipation in your newsletter by talking about things related to your upcoming product.

Let's say you've got a new eBook on the way about how to boost productivity. In one of your newsletters, you could cover how much of an issue productivity is, and how it slows us all down. That's just an example. Feel free to come up with your own.

And, if you manage to create a fever pitch buzz, you might find your subscribers start sharing your exciting news with others. You'll be amazed at how quickly news spreads.

Pulling The Emotional Triggers
Marketers have to keep pulling the emotional triggers, because it's only once they've tapped into a prospects emotions and discovered a way of making them feel a certain way that they can go on to clinch the deal.

Take scarcity for example. If you tell people that an offer is only available for a limited amount of time, or that there are only 20 seats available for your webinar, you'll create a feeling of urgency, and even one of panic. Fearing they might miss out (FOMO is real), people will clamor to sign up as soon as possible.

Naturally, it's not enough you say, "Sign up today before the price goes up!" There still needs to be a convincing reason as to why someone should sign up.

Scarcity is a hugely powerful motivator that resonates with every person. What if they miss out on this once in a lifetime opportunity and their neighbor gets it instead? What if their life improves because of this service, while yours stay the same? Handle this emotional trigger ethically, and you're on to a winner.

Another emotion you really need to tap into is curiosity.

Let's face it, people all love a sneaky peak. When an episode of your favorite drama series ends, you stay for the "Next time …" preview. Everyone loves it. It builds the excitement. People by their nature are curious. In fact, when it comes down to it, people are just as curious as cats. Pulling this particular emotional trigger means you can entice new customers over, while making existing prospects giddy. Get people in the mood. Give them a reason to keep checking their emails for updates!

CHAPTER 3: ETHICAL BRIBES

Don't fret, this isn't the illegal kind. The kind of bribe mentioned here is what is known as an ethical bribe. In other words, it's not about dishonesty.

Remember the Agora Model? In the Agora Model, you offer your subscribers something for free in return for them signing up to your emailing list. It has to be something relevant to your target audience, and which will therefore appeal to everyone. You need to be as creative as possible with what you offer to give away for free.

After all, people are giving you their email addresses and inviting you to come into their inbox a few times a week with your newsletters, promotions, surveys, and so on. It's a big deal. As such, they accept something premium in return. They want something of value.

This might be hard to get your head around at first. "Why would I give something premium away for FREE?" It's part of the bribe. People won't do their bit unless you do your bit. And don't be so precious about what you're giving away. Remember, all entrepreneurs give loads of stuff away for free. In fact, they give away most of their stuff for free.

Why? Because they know the value in it. They know that in helping them amass more followers, the free stuff is creating lots more value. It's creating an audience that they can sell to later on. So, yes, you're technically bribing people. But it's an ethical bribe. There is certainly nothing wrong with it.

Aim For Stuff That Could Go Viral

What do all marketers want on the Internet? They want to go viral. When you go viral, you achieve Internet fame. Your name in the Internet Hall of Fame is assured! Thousands - maybe even millions - of people know all about you and your product. Everyone knows your name, your Instagram account, your twitter account, and so on.

Most marketers will tell you that there is no magic formula to going viral. There is no recipe that's going to do the trick. What goes viral is purely down to luck. In some ways, they're right. But in some ways, they're wrong.

You can't second-guess what's going to go viral. But you can do certain things that will improve the odds of you coming up with content that's got the potential to get shared all over the Internet.

For example, freebies. People love freebies. If you say, "Share this post for a chance to win" you've got a better chance of said post going viral.

Bob Bly is a man who is worth listening to when it comes to any kind of marketing. He's written over 75 books, and he knows what he's talking about. He says that more than 80% of people will forward emails that have a special offer. They will share the email with friends and family, and anyone else then can think of who would find it useful.

Free Info Or Premium Solutions For Free?
Ask yourself what would you rather have? Would you rather have some free information ... or would you rather have a premium solution for free?

If you're like everyone else, you'd take the latter all day long. Rather than simply give something away, you could instead off up a solution to your customers' problem.

For example, your premium product could be a tutorial that walks people through the steps needed to complete a task, or it could be a checklist that helps them to identify what they need to do and when in order to solve a problem. Your premium product might even be an industry-related guide.

Whatever it is, it needs to have what is known as a high-perceived value. This means it's worth so much in the prospects eyes that - if push came to shove - they would happily pay for it. Any product that has a high-perceived value encourages more of the right people to opt-into your newsletter.

Like it or not, there will be people who opt-into your list just to get their hands on that freebie. It's the way things are. They're not interested in what you've got to say, whether you're an authority in your niche, or whether you're going to address their long-term problem. They just want that free gift. As such, they might even opt-out as soon as they've got it.

And just incase you're worried that your free premium product will give away all your secrets, if it does, you clearly don't have many secrets! The real concern you should have is how premium your product is.

See, if you're advertising something as premium, you have to deliver. This is essential. No one who pays for lemonade and gets tap water is going to be satisfied.

"But they're not PAYING for anything!" you might protest. Quit with that attitude. Get out of that mindset. Your free premium product should be good enough and enticing enough that they want more of where it came from.

Promote A Free Solution
Once you've decided what your bargaining chip is going to be that will incentivize people to sign-up, the hard work starts.

It's not enough that you say, "Hey! I've got some free stuff on my website!" Who are you talking to? You now need to find way of maximizing your sign-up incentive's exposure. In other words, you need to promote it.

You could start with a self-explanatory, targeted URL. This is always a good start. It must be related to the product, and it must be simple to read.

For example, let's say you're giving a book away called How To Write Faster. The URL could be the name of your website followed by how-to-write-faster.

If you're good at networking and often going to events and meeting people, you could advertise your free product in person. Why not? Simply go to an appropriate networking event and casually drop your offer into a conversation. This is where having a simple, easy to find URL matters. You can just write it out on a napkin and hand it out.

You should also start including the link to your opt-in page in your email signature. Everyone else does, so why aren't you? It means that anytime someone receives an email from you, there is a link right there to your awesome free product. If it sounds like something they'd love, they'll for sure be clicking.

And how about this one? Remove the link to your website in your social media bio, and instead add the link to your opt-in page. This is a great tactic that only the pro email marketers are using. It's a bit of a secret tip. And now you know it, too!

Finally, there is your website, too. But just incase you haven't done so already, make sure the link is in a good spot where everyone can see it. Don't put it at the bottom where people might not even look. Be smart about it.

Share Your Free Gift With Other Marketers
"Wait a minute. Why should you share your free gift with other marketers? Why should you help them build their audience?" You do something for them, and they'll do something for you.

Let's say a fellow marketer has a similar target audience as you. The only difference is that theirs is bigger. A LOT bigger.

So why not ask the marketer if they can invite their audience to opt-into your newsletter by sharing with them your free gift? The only problem with this one is that other marketers might not go for it. They might turn you down.

To improve the chances of them partnering up with you, offer to return the favor by promoting one of their products. They still might turn you down if you don't have a big enough audience yet. If so, just offer to give them the free gift full stop. Let them give it away.

Okay, so this means their audience won't come to your opt-in page. But they will see your message once they open the gift. Again, you've just got to be smart and be prepared to hustle.

Brand The Solution Like A Pro
Let's imagine that people who receive your gift are going to share it with others. For you, this is free advertising. Awesome!

But since you're going to be shared on the Internet, you first of all need to make sure that your brand is on-point. In other words, make sure your free gift does a great job at selling you, your company, and its products. Don't give away a lousy product that is rubbish. Give something away that's going to raise your profile and advertise your brand.

CHAPTER 4: CROSS-SUBSIDY MARKETING

"Cross subsidy marketing is the improper assignment of costs among objects such that certain objects are over-costed while other cost objects are under-costed."

What does that mean?

Admittedly, it sounds nonsensical but translated into simple marketing lingo, it means that if you've got a great selection of digital goods on your hands, an easy email marketing tactic would be to give something away for free in exchange for your customers buying something else from you.

Basically, people will only get a freebie from you if they're willing to buy your brand new product. You might be thinking, "But this sounds hard. Why would anyone snap something up for free if they've still got to spend money on something else anyway?" It's actually easier than it sounds.

Tactical Cross-Subsidies
Putting together a tactical cross-subsidy admittedly sounds a bit tricky at this point. It sounds hard. But so do most things when you first start them.

After a few attempts, putting together a tactical cross-subsidy will become second nature to you, too.

Here's an example:

A year or so ago, a company launched a paperback version of one of their eBooks. They launched it a fair few months after they had put out the eBook version and offered it on Amazon.

The thing is, nobody was aware of its existence. As such, it didn't sell. It was ranked 200,000 in its particular niche. Either people were seeing it and didn't want it, or nobody was searching for it.

So what the company did was they included an eye-catching special offer in one of their newsletters. They sent this newsletter to around 20,000 subscribers and it read as follows:

"Free Coupon For A Strictly Limited Time Only! We are happy to announce that we are now releasing our popular eBook as a paperback that you can hold in your hands. Lots of you have been inquiring as to when the paperback version will be launched, and we're thrilled that it's finally here. We've been waiting for this day for a long time! Because we're thankful for your tremendous support, we're offering a coupon equivalent

to $15.00 for FREE products of your choosing on our website if you buy our book. Help us nudge into the bestsellers list and grab your coupon while it's hot."

What the company did was offer $15 worth of their stock for anyone who bought the book. That's a pretty good deal. They also added the "limited time only" line in there because they know it creates a sense of urgency and causes people to act fast.

And because all their stock was digital, it meant that it didn't technically cost them anything - cash or time. There were no postage and packaging charges, and they didn't have to spend any time preparing to send stuff out to people. They just chose their product, hit the download button, and boom! All done.

Our cross-subsidy tactic caused people to act. It made them think, "Why on earth wouldn't I take them up on this offer?" It was a no-brainer and too good to ignore.

Not everyone took up the offer, of course. But lots of people did, and they helped to rocket the book from #200,000 to #2,100 in just two weeks. And it all came from one easy-to-put-together email.

CHAPTER 5: STYLE POINTS

One aspect of email marketing that many marketers dread is the writing process. Lots of marketers dread it because they're not writers. They're marketers! But just like a freelance writer needs to learn the ropes of marketing, you as a marketer need to learn the ropes of writing.

You don't need a literary degree but you just need to be able to communicate your message in a friendly, positive tone that engages your reader, interacts with them, informs them and entertains them.

Here are some tips you can follow:

Be Friendly
Now, even though you're already a friendly person by nature, that doesn't mean it's going to come across in your writing - especially if you're nervous.

When you first start writing, it can be easy to get struck down with nerves and lose confidence. In such circumstances, you just want to bash the words out and relay your message. And when this happens, oftentimes you forget to be friendly and your tone becomes unapproachable. Unless you can establish, a friendly, personable tone, you will struggle to win people over. You will struggle to get them to trust you. Harsh, but true.

So, quit the dry language. Stop talking about your product and its features. Open up. Be conversational. Say hi! Make a comment on the weather. Empathize with your reader. Talk to them like you would a friend.

At the same time, though, it's important you don't overdo it. It's a balancing act. If you try to be too friendly, you'll forget why you're even here in the first place and your message will get lost. But it's important that your tone remains friendly and personable throughout your emails. Be likeable.

Using The Newsletter Format
Don't go into this without using a template. If you do, your emails won't look very structured.

Using the newsletter format/template gives your emails some structure, and helps to guide your readers' eye. They know this is a newsletter.

Your email provider should have a few nice-looking templates for you to choose from. Check them out and see which ones work best for you. Once you've picked one and created your first newsletter, you can then duplicate it and use it over and over again. It's easy and efficient.

It will take you a bit of time to create the look you want, and you might even find that you tweak it after you've already sent out a few emails. But that's okay. Polishing a newsletter will take a bit of effort. But once it's done, it's done!

Using The Simple Text Format
Why use the simple text format? When you do, your email will look just like any other email - which is what you want. All you do is add an introductory Hello, such as "Hey guys and girls," before proceeding with the bulk of your message.

Using HTML Formatting
Look, you could send an email without HTML formatting. Email providers let you do that, and some giddy newbie email marketers take them up on the offer. But it's a massive mistake.

Why? Because without HTML formatting you won't be able to track your results. You won't know your click-through rates. In other words, you won't know how successful a campaign is. Plain-text emails are a bit more personal, and feel like the kind of email you normally receive from someone you know. A text-based email is ideal if you're targeting information seekers. These people just want something that gets straight to the point. They don't want any fancy imagery or graphics.

Then there is HTML, which is perfect for visuals and branding. It's the format most used by companies.

If you want the best of HTML and text-based, it's recommended that you go for text which is in an HTML shell. It looks a lot like plain text, yet it acts more like HTML. Crucially, it can also be monitored like HTML. At the same time, it also lets you use cool graphics and fonts.

Check Out Mail Chimp

So many email marketers swear by Mail Chimp. If you're totally new to the world of email marketing, it's a good idea to start using Mail Chimp. Why? Because it makes your life so much easier. Even better, you get its services for free until you surpass 2,000 subscribers. That's a good deal.

Skimmers Want Easy Reading

When you're reading a magazine you just paid $8 for, you will of course read the articles in full. You certainly won't skim through the whole thing in a race to get to the end. But emails are totally different. And many of us - you included, perhaps - tend to skim.

Therefore, you need to make sure your emails are readable. Hook them in with catchy subtitles, break key points down into bullet points, and use short paragraphs.

If a subscriber is confronted with massive blocks of paragraphs and no subtitles, they're probably not going to waste their time reading it.

People are busy. They haven't got time for your novel. Break things up. Use orientation points to guide them. Make it easy for them to find the info they're looking for. The most important thing here is that you keep them on the page with snappy text that looks easy to read.

Keep your paragraphs concise. Use short sentences. Use punchy language. Include subheadings that let readers know exactly what's coming in each paragraph. Stay focused on the message. Don't go off on a tangent about this or that. Stick to just that one message. Keep things simple if you want to keep readers on the page.

Leverage Everything You've Got

Make the most of every single part of your email, from the body to the subject line. It's important, and it plays a crucial role in hooking your audience and getting them to click, read and take action.

It all starts with your subject line, which is after all the first thing any reader sees. The body might be fabulous. But they're not going to make it that far if the subject line doesn't get them interested.

Your subject line needs to be short and engaging. It should be no longer than 40 characters, and it needs to be unique, urgent, useful and ultra-specific. Those are your four U's, and all of them are important.

You should also use trigger words that make people compelled to open the email, such as "Free" and "Cash." These are emotive words that are highly effective at making readers feel a certain way.

Imagine if you told someone that your product could make them X amount of cash in just seven days? They'd feel pretty great! At the least they would be curious enough to click on the email. However, these trigger words are also susceptible to spam-filters, so be careful. The last thing you want is for some spam filter to filter them and your whole email out.

Next up, you need to make sure that your "From" line is clear as daylight. Who is sending this? You? How do they know it's you? Don't make the mistake of being vague here. If they're not sure who is sending the email, why should they open it?

Then there is the small matter of your headline. This will be similar to your subject line, and needs to be just as compelling. It sits at the top of your newsletter, and needs to address exactly why the reader should keep on reading. What's in store for them? What key piece of info are they going to take away? What value are they going to get from reading this? Crafting headlines isn't easy and it takes time.

Next is your lead-in sentence, which is the first sentence. Journalists call it the hook, and you may as well borrow that phrase. Because essentially your first sentence needs to hook your reader and reel 'em in! As such, it's got to be good. Maybe you could ask a question that identifies a particular pain point they have, such as "Are you fed up with never sleeping and going into work tired?"

Get down to the action immediately with the first sentence. Grab their attention. You literally have one second to do so.

A key part of your email you need to consider but which a lot of newbie email marketers overlook is the margins. If you don't get your margins just right, your newsletter might look cluttered and hard to read. Margins are especially important if you use design elements, such as photos and sidebars.

Lastly, there is the opt-out. To achieve credibility and trust, you MUST include the option for your subscribers to unsubscribe. Otherwise, they might feel anxious that they're stuck here. The opt-out option is actually a legal requirement, so you need to include it anyway. But it's also important for trust. Also, you'll want to know why people are opting out so that you can produce better content. You can do this by including a form that asks people for their reason(s).

Writing Interesting Stories, Being Funny Or Offering Wisdom

There will come a time when you will feel as if you've run out of ideas and literally don't know what the heck to include in your newsletter.

Just how do you keep things interesting for so long? It's always a good idea to include a story or a humorous idea, or even a cool new business concept.

If you do decide to tell a story, make sure it has some relevance to your business.

Or maybe you could highlight something in your industry that might seem obvious to you, but which won't be so obvious to your reader. Use your own experiences and write about them. The things that have happened to you will be so ingrained in your mind that you might think they'd make boring stories. But while they're old stories to you, they're new ones to the rest of your readers. And they would love to hear them!

Always remember that you're the expert here, and that your readers are - by and large - total novices in comparison. They don't know nearly as much as you do, but they have a thirst to learn. Use your position as the authority figure and expert to your advantage here. Don't just try to sell stuff all the time. Make some effort to educate your subscribers. They'll appreciate it.

If you're still unable to come up with any ideas, take the time to sit down and make a list of the questions you think prospect and customers have about your company. Put yourself in their shoes and ask what would YOU like to know about your company.

It's like Ask The Expert. Customers have a fantastic chance to ask an expert a question. What would they ask? If you can come up with enough questions and answers, you should then have enough ideas for content that will keep you going for a few weeks.

If you've decided you're going to put out a daily newsletter, then the quest for content becomes even harder. Keeping things fresh is hard and constantly putting out your own content each day will prove to be both a thankless and a near impossible task.

As such, it's recommended that you look for outside sources. You could, for example, link your subscribers to relevant articles that you think would be useful. This is similar to when you retweet stuff that you think would be useful to your followers. It saves you from having to keep coming up with fresh, original content, but it also ensures your subscriber is still getting a good deal.

Develop Win-Win Situations
What's the greatest type of marketing? It's the type that develops win-win situations. You win, and so does the customer. Everyone leaves with a smile on their face. Happy days!

It's your job now to find a way of developing those win-win situations all the time. You want to create a Paradise Factory, where everyone is a winner. You want to create the feel good factor and keep it going!

Here's how one company did it:

A couple of years ago, they released a successful eBook and published it on Amazon. Taking their cue from Guy Kawasaki, they implemented a number of strategies. For starters, they signed up for KDP (Kindle Direct Publishing). This is free and it means you can list your book for FREE for 5 days (they don't have to be consecutive) ever ninety days.

You might be skeptical. Why would you list your book for free? What if all your prospects snap it up for free in those 5 days and no one is left to buy it? Won't happen. Never happens.

On the contrary, listing your book for 5 days gives it an incredible amount of exposure. People see it. They download it. They take a chance they probably wouldn't have taken had it not been for free. Their book rocketed up the free book chart, until eventually it was on page one.

But they still wanted to make their subscribers happy, and they still wanted to leverage their emailing list.

So they wrote an email - just a brief, simple one - and sent it out to their list a day before the new book was available to download. The email reached the near 2,000 people who had subscribed to stay up-to-date with it.

The company told them that it would be free for the next twenty-four hours, after which the price would go up to $12. They asked them if they could do the company a massive favor by downloading it, reading it, reviewing it and - if they liked it - recommending it to a friend. They then made sure to include the link.

And you know what? People acted. They downloaded. The book was propelled up to #40 in ALL free Kindle eBooks. That meant huge exposure, and it was even #1 in a few categories.

They kept the momentum going. People reviewed it, which gave it some much-needed credibility (without reviews, your eBook is not going to sell well at all).

After that initial, feverish twenty-four hour window, the book returned to its normal price. Because of the buzz they had already created, it continued to sell.

They were happy, and their customers definitely seemed happy. They'd gotten a free book and they loved it!

CHAPTER 6: EFFECTIVE CLICK THROUGHS AND OPEN RATES

Click-through and open rates are marketing jargon that refers to how many people are opening your emails and then clicking on links. Your email provider should provide you with an analytic tool that will help you to track both statistics. It's a useful tool to have, as it lets you know how well your email campaign is performing.

Make A Buddy With Mobile
Do you know how your subscribers are going to be reading your email? In other words, what devices will they be using?

They'll probably open your emails on their mobile phone. Maybe they'll open them on their tablet or maybe they'll open them on their computer. But in all likelihood, they'll be opening them on their phones.

This will be a major problem for you if your email template isn't mobile-ready. And as surprising as it may sound to you, lots of newbie email marketers don't consider this. Their templates just aren't mobile ready, which stops readers from engaging with your content.

Mobile usage is increasing, and for the first time ever has finally overtaken desktop. It was always predicted that this would happen, and it finally has. If you don't make your email templates mobile-ready, this is bad news for your business. Email marketing is heading to mobile. Make sure you don't lose out.

Master Your Open Rates
Your open rates are the best indicator of how successful your marketing campaign is. It lets you know how many emails have been opened - and how many haven't. In other words, it lets you know whether there are things that need tweaking.

For example, if your open rates are excellent, there's no reason to tweak your subject line. It's clearly working, and they always say that you shouldn't fix what isn't broken. However, if your open rates are awful, it's time to carry out some maintenance work.

The one problem with open rates is that you can never be sure how accurate they are. They're rarely 100% accurate because they rely on an invisible image that acts as a tracker. Unfortunately, some email programs choose to block images!

Open rates vary, but they tend to fall in a rather narrow ballpark between 16 and 27%.

These numbers might not seem amazing, but they're normal. You certainly shouldn't go into your campaign expecting yours to be much higher. Remember that you've got a margin of error here, and that each business gets bounces - even the best marketers have bounces!

Moreover, if you don't like your open rate, simply make it your goal to beat it each week or month. Experiment with different approaches. Try a different subject line. Come up with different content.

Usually, it's the subject line that trips us up. The subject line is the first thing that a reader sees. If it's not juicy, compelling or informative, they're probably not going to open it. Why should they waste their time?

Targeted content is something else you need to consider. By this you should take a look at your analytics and find out which types of content are scoring the best open rates, and which ones are scoring the worst. Then, you can start focusing on the best ones while ditching the others.

Then there is the follow-through. You promised something in the subject line. But are you delivering it?

Re-engagement is a time-sucker, but you need to consider it. Take some time to find out who hasn't opened one of your emails in months. Then, create a campaign specifically for them with the aim of getting them back on board. If this seems like too much work, just kick them from your list. Otherwise, they're just dragging your numbers down.

Now, just because someone has opened your emails, you shouldn't then take it as a given that they've actually enjoyed reading them. Be realistic about your campaign. Not everyone who opens one of your emails is going to engage with them. Some will, sure. But not all will.

But how do you find out how much value or enjoyment a person is getting out of your emails? It's hard to determine exactly, but you can get a rough idea by looking at your unsubscribe and bounce rates.

Your bounce rate reflects the amount of emails that haven't reached the recipients. This could be for any number of reasons, but the most likely reason is that a spam filter got in the way.

Your unsubscribe rate is self-explanatory. People WILL unsubscribe from you. That's a given. Try not to lose heart when they do. Just accept it and then try to improve your customer experience so that you give your subscribers more of what they want and less of what they don't want.

A low unsubscribe rate that stays fairly stable is normal. But instead of letting it discourage you, you should let it motivate you to do better and better. If there is a sudden spike in your unsubscribe rate, it should act as a wake-up call that whatever it is you've been doing recently just isn't working.

Responsiveness Is A Better Indicator Of Success Than Big

Think having a huge emailing list is the best measure of success? Think again. The surest indicator of success right now is how responsive your list of subscribers are. It's much better to have a small list of people who respond (engage and interact) with your content then a massive list of people who barely respond at all.

Big whoop, you got a big list! "LOOK AT ME AND MY 20,000 SUBSCRIBERS!" It doesn't mean a thing if just .5% of them are responsive. Moreover, maintaining that huge list of unresponsive subscribers is draining your resources. You need to focus on getting yourself a small, tight group of responsive subscribers who care about your content and products.

Make A Hell Week

The final tip is that you should put your new subscribers through the email-marketing equivalent of Hell Week. The goal? To separate the wheat from the chaff. In other words, to filter out those newbies who aren't committed.

On the first day, you should send out your Welcome Email. This should explain what they can expect in the week ahead. On the second day, include a special note, which introduces your story about how and why you founded your business. On the third day, talk about your main service or product. On the fourth day, talk about your team and the qualifications you each have. On the fifth day, talk about your company's values, vision and mission. On the sixth day, talk about your special offers and annual sales. On the seventh day, reward your readers with a coupon or a free gift.

The aim of this is to weed out those who clearly aren't interested in you and what you have to offer. You want them to leave.

CONCLUSION

A lot of people say that email marketing is hard. Often, it takes them three or four attempts before they finally get it right.

Hopefully, the advice and the strategies in this book have made things a lot clearer for you, and helped you learn how you can take your business from strength to strength.

Happy emailing!

THANKS FOR READING

We really hope you enjoyed this book. If you found this material helpful feel free to share it with friends. You can also help others find it by leaving a review where you purchased the book. Your feedback will help us continue to write books you love.

The Smart Reads library is growing by the day! Make sure and check out the other wonderful books in our catalog. We would love to hear which books are your favorite.

Visit:
www.smartreads.co/freebooks
to receive Smart Reads books for FREE

Check us out on Instagram:
www.instagram.com/smart_readers
@smart_readers

Don't forget your 2 FREE audiobooks.
Use this link www.audibletrial.com/Travis to claim
your 2 FREE Books.

SMART READS ORIGINS

Smart Reads was born out of the desire to find the best information fast without having to wade through the sheer volume of fluff available online. Smart Reads combs through massive amounts of knowledge compiles the best into quick to read books on a variety of subjects.

We consider ourselves Smart Readers, not dummies. We know reading is smart. We're self taught. We like to learn a TON about a WIDE variety of topics. We have developed a love for books and we find intelligence attractive.

We found that each new topic we tried to learn about started with the challenge of finding the pieces of the puzzle that mattered most. It becomes a treasure hunt rather than an education.

Smart Reads wants to find the best of the best information for you. To condense it into a package that you can consume in an hour or less. So you can read more books about more topics in less time.

OUR MISSION

Smart Reads aims to accelerate the availability of useful information and will publish a high quality book on every major topic on amazon.

Smart Reads hopes to remove barriers to sharing by taking the copyright off everything we publish and donating it to the public domain. We hope other publishers and authors will follow our example.

Our goal is to donate $1,000,000 or more by 2020 to build over 2,000 schools by giving 5% of our net profit to Pencils of Promise.

We want to restore forests around the globe by planting a tree for every 10 physical books we sell and hope to plant over 100,000 trees by 2020.

Doesn't it feel good knowing that by educating yourself you are helping the world be a better place? We think so too...

Thanks for helping us help the world. You Smart Reader you...

Travis and the Smart Reads Team

WHY I STARTED SMART READS

Every time I wanted to learn about something new I'd have to buy 20 books on the topic and spend way too long sorting through them and reading them all until I arrived at the big picture. Until I had enough perspectives to know who was just guessing, who was uninformed and who had stumbled upon something remarkable.

I wished someone else could just go in and figure that out for me and tell me what matters. That's how smart reads was born. I want smart reads to be a company that does all that research up front. Sorts through all the content that is available on each topic and pulls out the most up to date complete understanding, then have people smarter than me package the best wisdom in an easy to understand way in the least amount of words possible.

For example, I got a new puppy so I wanted to learn about dog training. I bought 14 different books about dog training and by the time I got through the first 5 and finally started getting the big picture on the best way to train my puppy she had grown up into a dog.

Yeah she's well behaved. She doesn't poop in the house. I can get her to sit and come when I call. But what if someone else went in and read all those books for me, found the underlying themes and picked out the best information that would give me the big picture and get me right to the point. And I'd only have to read one book instead of 15.

That would be amazing. I would save time. And maybe my dog would be rolling over, cleaning up after my kids and doing the dishes by now. That my friend, is the reason I started smart reads. Because I wanted a company I can trust to deliver me the best information in an easy to understand way that I can digest in under an hour. Because dog training is one of many subjects I want to master.

The quicker I can learn a wide variety of topics the sooner that information can begin playing a role in shaping my future. And none of us knows how long that future will be. So why not do everything we can to make the best of it and consume a ton of knowledge. And I figured all the better if I can also make a positive difference in the world.

That's why we're also building schools, planting trees and challenging ideas about copyright's place in today's world. Because as a company we have to be doing everything we can to support the ecosystem that gives us all these beautiful places to read our books. Thanks for reading.

Travis

Customers Who Bought This Customers Who Bought This Book Also Bought

Email Marketing 101: How to Gain Subscribers, Grow Your List and Make Sales

Twitter Marketing Strategies: Smart Tips on How to Monetize Your Followers

Passive Income: Do What You Want When You Want and Make Money While You Sleep

Reinvent Yourself: Become Instantly Likable, Captivate Anyone in Seconds and Always Know What To Say

How to Master Email Marketing: Your 1-Page Marketing Plan to Grow a Massive Email List, Make Money and Build Your Brand with Email

Writing on the Internet: Learn SEO Tips &
Techniques and Become a Successful Online
Writer

The Art of Coaching: How to Explain Clearly and
Become a Good Leader